THE FREEDOM OF CHRISTIAN LIVING

ROMANS 12-16

7 INTERACTIVE BIBLE STUDIES FOR
SMALL GROUPS AND INDIVIDUALS

GORDON CHENG

matthiasmedia

The Freedom of Christian Living
© Matthias Media 2009

Matthias Media
(St Matthias Press Ltd ACN 067 558 365)
PO Box 225
Kingsford NSW 2032
Australia
Telephone: (02) 9663 1478; international: +61-2-9663-1478
Facsimile: (02) 9663 3265; international: +61-2-9663-3265
Email: info@matthiasmedia.com.au
Internet: www.matthiasmedia.com.au

Matthias Media (USA)
Telephone: 724 964 8152; international: +1-724-964-8152
Facsimile: 724 964 8166; international: +1-724-964-8166
Email: sales@matthiasmedia.com
Internet: www.matthiasmedia.com

Scripture quotations are from The Holy Bible, English Standard Version, copyright © 2001 by Crossway Bibles, a publishing ministry of Good News Publishers. Used by permission. All rights reserved.

ISBN 978 1 921441 40 0

All rights reserved. Except as may be permitted by the Copyright Act, no part of this publication may be reproduced in any form or by any means without prior permission from the publisher.

Cover design and typesetting by Lankshear Design Pty Ltd.

» CONTENTS

How to make the most of these studies 5

STUDY 1: Transform your life
           [Romans 12:1-8] 9

STUDY 2: Lovers not fighters
           [Romans 12:9-21] 15

STUDY 3: Reasons for living righteously
           [Romans 13] 21

STUDY 4: Freedom perfected
           [Romans 14] 29

STUDY 5: The end of weakness and strength
           [Romans 15:1-13] 37

STUDY 6: God bless America (and everyone else)
           [Romans 15:14-33] 45

STUDY 7: Friends and enemies
           [Romans 16] 51

ROMANS 12-16

»HOW TO MAKE THE MOST OF THESE STUDIES

1. What is an Interactive Bible Study?

Interactive Bible Studies are a bit like a guided tour of a famous city. They take you through a particular part of the Bible, helping you to know where to start, pointing out things along the way, suggesting avenues for further exploration, and making sure that you know how to get home. Like any good tour, the real purpose is to allow you to go exploring for yourself—to dive in, have a good look around, and discover for yourself the riches that God's word has in store.

In other words, these studies aim to provide stimulation and input and point you in the right direction, while leaving you to do plenty of the exploration and discovery yourself.

We hope that these studies will stimulate lots of 'interaction'—interaction with the Bible, with the things we've written, with your own current thoughts and attitudes, with other people as you discuss them, and with God as you talk to him about it all.

2. The format

Each study contains five main components:
- short sections of text that introduce, inform, summarize and challenge
- a set of numbered study questions that help you examine the passage and think through its meaning
- sidebars that provide extra bits of background or optional extra study ideas, especially regarding other relevant parts of the Bible
- an 'Implications' section that helps you think about what this passage means for you and your life today
- suggestions for thanksgiving and prayer as you close.

3. How to use these studies on your own

- Before you begin, pray that God would open your eyes to what he is saying in the Bible, and give you the spiritual strength to do something about it.
- Work through the study, reading the text, answering the questions about the Bible passage, and exploring the sidebars as you have time.
- Resist the temptation to skip over the 'Implications' and 'Give thanks and pray' sections at the end. It is important that we not only hear and understand God's word, but respond to it. These closing sections help us do that.
- Take what opportunities you can to talk to others about what you've learnt.

4. How to use these studies in a small group

- Much of the above applies to group study as well. The studies are suitable for structured Bible study or cell groups, as well as for more informal pairs and triplets. Get together with a friend or friends and work through them at your own pace; use them as the basis for regular Bible study with your spouse. You don't need the formal structure of a 'group' to gain maximum benefit.

- For small groups, it is *very useful* if group members can work through the study themselves *before* the group meets. The group discussion can take place comfortably in an hour (depending on how side-tracked you get!) if all the members have done some work in advance.
- The role of the group leader is to direct the course of the discussion and to try to draw the threads together at the end. This will mean a little extra preparation—underlining the sections of text to emphasize and read out loud, working out which questions are worth concentrating on, and being sure of the main thrust of the study. Leaders will also probably want to work out approximately how long they'd like to spend on each part.
- If your group members usually don't work through the study in advance, it's extra important that the leader prepares which parts to concentrate on, and which parts to glide past more quickly. In particular, the leader will need to select which of the 'Implications' to focus on.
- We haven't included an 'answer guide' to the questions in the studies. This is a deliberate move. We want to give you a guided tour of the Bible, not a lecture. There is more than enough in the text we have written and the questions we have asked to point you in what we think is the right direction. The rest is up to you.

5. Bible translation

Previous studies in our Interactive Bible Study series have assumed that most readers would be using the New International Version of the Bible. However, since the release of the English Standard Version in 2001, many have switched to the ESV for study purposes. For this reason, we have decided to quote from and refer to the ESV text, which we recommend.

STUDY 1

TRANSFORM YOUR LIFE

[ROMANS 12:1-8]

These days there is an impressive industry in life coaching. If you are struggling with weight gain or with fitness, you don't have to go to the gym alone, or even with a friend. You can engage your own personal trainer. And it doesn't stop there. The personal-advice industry can also help you with diet, finance, relationships and goal setting. If you lose your job, they can even help you become a life coach!

What is the Bible's view on how to change? And what is the goal of that change? Romans 12 has a lot to say on change and 'transformation', but it is not the self-focused type of change being promoted by the life-coaching industry. It is a transformation that begins with God, focuses on other people, and results in glory not to people but to God himself.

What the 'therefore' is there for

It's a basic rule of understanding when you are reading an argument: the first thing you must do when you stumble upon a 'therefore' is ask yourself, "What is it there for?" We meet one such 'therefore' in Romans 12:1, when Paul says "I appeal to you *therefore*, brothers, by the mercies of God, to present your bodies as a living sacrifice ..."

Paul has been talking about God's mercy in the verses immediately before this passage. In particular, he has been talking about how God has shown mercy to the Gentiles, and will again show mercy to Israel. So in one sense, the 'therefore' picks up these "mercies of God" from chapter 11. But the summary of God's mercies to both Jew and Gentile in chapter 11 is really the climax of Paul's whole argument in Romans.

Paul started back in chapter 1 with an explanation of God's righteousness (note the verse that sets out Paul's theme, Romans 1:17: "For in it [that is, the gospel] the righteousness of God is revealed from faith for faith, as it is written, 'The righteous shall live by faith'"), and then moved on to its implications. Those implications are massive—for the Christian life, which is by faith; for the law, which has been satisfied; for the future, ▶

Read Romans 12:1-3.

1. Consider the word 'sacrifice' in verse 1.

   a. Is Paul talking about offering sacrifice for sin? Why or why not? (Compare Romans 3:21-26.)

   b. What normally happens to sacrifices? (For an example, see Leviticus 3:1-5.)

   c. Given your answer to question 1b, what does it mean to be a "living sacrifice"?

d. In the Old Testament, Israel offered **'worship'** and 'sacrifice' in the temple. Where do we 'worship' and offer sacrifice today?

2. What do you think it means to be "conformed to this world":

a. at work?

b. in your family?

c. in your daily routine?

d. at church?

because nothing is "able to separate us from the love of God in Christ Jesus our Lord" (Rom 8:39). Chapters 9-11 show that God remains righteous, even though his promises to the Jews seem, at first, to have failed. Indeed, the Gentiles especially must realize that the *true* Jews have certainly not been rejected, and in the triumphant purposes of God, both Jew and Gentile will end up praising him together. The instructions to transformed living in Romans 12-16 flow directly out of the mercies of God in Christ. In other words, everything that follows is a response to God's goodness and righteousness, not an attempt to win his favour.

Worship

The Old and New Testaments use a number of different Hebrew and Greek words to describe the act of 'worship', but the heart of the idea is making a fitting response to God, sometimes expressed in a direct physical way by bowing down before him (e.g. Genesis 24:52, where the word 'bowed' could equally well be translated as 'worshipped'). In the rest of the Old Testament, especially in Exodus, Leviticus, Numbers and Deuteronomy, God sets out the right way to worship him—at the temple, controlled by the priests, and in accordance with the sacrificial system. ▶

However, this was never meant to be simply a matter of external ritual, and later Old Testament prophets criticized Israel again and again for their failure to match their lives with their worship. God complains through Isaiah:

> "What to me is the multitude of
>   your sacrifices?
>   says the Lord;
> I have had enough of burnt offerings
>   of rams
>   and the fat of well-fed beasts;
> I do not delight in the blood of bulls,
>   or of lambs, or of goats.
>
> "When you come to appear before me,
>   who has required of you
> this trampling of my courts?"
>   (Isa 1:11-12)

In other words, true worship has never been simply a matter of performing the right rituals in the right location. As King David says, "The sacrifices of God are a broken spirit; a broken and contrite heart, O God, you will not despise" (Ps 51:17). Verses like these lie behind Paul's exhortations to *spiritual* worship.

3. How does transformation take place?

4. Verse 2 assures us that when our minds are renewed, the result will be "that by testing you may discern what is the will of God, what is good and acceptable and perfect".

    a. What will this look like in practice? (Use verse 3 to work out one application.)

    b. What are some ways in which we are tempted to think too highly of ourselves?

Read Romans 12:4-8.

5. A renewed mind leads to a new way of thinking about ourselves. In verses 4-8, this then flows on to how we relate to others. What does the person with the renewed mind do with the gifts God has given?

6. How do these verses help the person who feels:

  a. inferior?

  b. superior?

The battle within

When Paul talks about being "transformed", he is not simply talking about behaviour change. That is far too easy! He is talking about a complete transformation of our lives, including our thinking. In fact, the renewal of our minds is the driving force behind the transformation of our lives.

All this presupposes a great battle, expressed in Romans 12:2 as a struggle between our desire to follow the "world", and our desire to "discern what is the will of God". Earlier in Romans, Paul makes us aware of this battle in other ways. So in Romans 6 we can be "slaves of sin" or "slaves of righteousness". In Romans 7, "I do not do the good I want". In Romans 8, the flesh and God's Spirit are at war within us. All of these perspectives remind us that the Christian life is not going to be an easy road to glory, but will involve a continual decision on our part to respond wholeheartedly to God's transforming mercy.

» Implications

- Paul commands us to "be transformed by the renewal of your mind", and has already spoken about how this can happen (e.g. Rom 6:12-13, 6:17 and 8:13-14). Reflect on what Paul says, and discuss how the "renewal of your mind" can become a daily practical reality.

- Christians often think of 'worship' as something that happens in church. What does Romans 12 have to say about this?

- Considering Paul's list of gifts in verses 6-8, what gifts has God given to you? What gifts has he given to others in your group? How will you use them to serve?

- What comfort can we offer to the person who says, "I didn't think the Christian life was going to be this hard!"?

» Give thanks and pray

- Thank God that we are transformed by his mercy.
- Pray that we will have a "sober judgement" about ourselves.
- Pray that we will use our gifts to serve others in the church.

STUDY 2
LOVERS NOT FIGHTERS
[ROMANS 12:9-21]

"Love means never having to say you're sorry." Or does it? Right at the beginning of this passage Paul twice commands people to "love".[1] "Let love be genuine", he tells us, and then as if to reinforce the message, "Love one another with brotherly affection".

So what exactly does Paul mean when he tells us that we are to love each other? The verses in this study give a practical outworking of what love might look like within a congregation. The hardest part of this study is not going to be working out complex and difficult details within the passage. The hardest part will be praying that God will help us do what he commands!

However, it is also worth remembering what Paul has already taught about the nature of love in the first 11 chapters of Romans. The verse which best sums it up is Romans 5:8, where Paul reminds us that "God shows his love for us in that while we were still sinners, Christ died for us". That is, if we are in any confusion at all about what love means, we need only look first to what God has done for us in Jesus. Because God loves us, he has acted by sending Jesus to die for our sins. So instead of the judgement we deserve, he has shown mercy. No wonder that Paul prefaces his instructions here in Romans 12 with the words "I appeal to you therefore, brothers, *by the mercies of God*" (v. 1).

1. We have already mentioned Romans 5:8. Now read the following verses from Romans,[2] and use them to write some short notes on how God shows his love for us:

- Romans 1:7

- Romans 5:5

- Romans 8:31-39

Read Romans 12:9-13.

2. How do these verses illustrate what 'love' means in practice?

3. For each member of the group: Pick one or more of Paul's instructions, and talk about how they challenge or help you personally to love other people.

Instruction	How you are challenged or helped (be specific)
Outdo one another in showing honour	
Do not be slothful in zeal, be fervent in spirit	
Rejoice in hope	
Be patient in tribulation	
Be constant in prayer	
Contribute to the needs of the saints and seek to show hospitality	

Read Romans 12:14–21.

4. Think about someone you hate, or who hates you (there's no need to name names!).

   a. What are you being commanded to do?

Vengeance is mine

There are some puzzling statements about vengeance in Romans 12. Deuteronomy 32:35 (quoted in Romans 12:19) makes sense, because in the context of Deuteronomy it is clear that God's enemies are being handed over to God's judgement, which is as it should be. Those enemies are disobedient members of the people of Israel, so it makes even more sense that it should be God who judges, and by the same token, that we have no right to do God's job for him. ▶

This is especially true when we are dealing with relationships within God's people, whether Israel in the Old Testament or the church in Rome.

More difficult is Romans 12:20, where the result of being kind to an enemy is that "you will heap burning coals on his head". Even allowing for picturesque language, this seems extreme, and some commentators have suggested that the burning coals are a metaphor for the enemy feeling ashamed when they are well-treated. But there is not much evidence for this view either in the passage, or for that matter in Proverbs 25:21-22, which is where the quote comes from.

Rather, as awkward as it seems to some modern readers, it is more likely that Paul is appealing to the justice of God. God will certainly bring judgement on his enemies, and Paul has already said this in Romans 1:18. Perhaps our squeamishness about the idea that God might indeed judge people is a problem we must come to terms with. As we do so, we may appreciate how this judgement can also serve as a comfort to people who have been wronged.

b. What might this look like in practice?

5. Think of someone you normally ignore. In this passage, what are you being commanded to do about them?

6. What reason(s) are we given for not taking revenge on people who hurt us?

7. Read Deuteronomy 32:34-43 and Proverbs 25:21-22 (the passages that are quoted in verses 19-20). What do these verses tell us about God's vengeance?

» Implications

- How has your belief in God affected how you relate to people you dislike or find hard to be with?

- Of all the exhortations in this passage, which do you find most personally challenging? What are you going to do about it?

- The idea of God's wrath (or vengeance) is not a popular one these days. Why is this, do you think? What do we lose when we lose sight of God's wrath?

» Give thanks and pray

- Pray for the people you thought about when you read this passage.
- Thank God that we can rely on him to bring justice.

Endnotes

1. The words are different in Greek, but both apply to the affection, respect, honour and cherishing that the Roman Christians are meant to show each other.
2. They are the other verses in Romans, up to this point, where 'love' is mentioned.

» STUDY 3

REASONS FOR LIVING RIGHTEOUSLY

[ROMANS 13]

In Romans 12, Paul began to speak about how we should treat each other in light of God's mercy to us. 'Love' was the biggest exhortation, and so far we have seen how love drives us towards zeal in service, and further, to humility, patience and kindness even to enemies.

But 'love' doesn't ever mean 'injustice'. Especially, it can't mean 'injustice' in the context of Romans, where Paul has insisted from the beginning of the letter that in the gospel "the *righteousness* of God is revealed" (Rom 1:16-17). He has explained, for example, how true love will include waiting patiently for God to exercise his judgement (see the previous study).

Now, in chapter 13 of Romans, we continue to think about how that righteousness of God is expressed in daily, practical Christian living—beginning with the way Christians treat those who govern.

Civil disobedience?

We live in an age where cynicism about government seems to be at an all-time high. Documentaries are produced criticizing government policy; officials, Presidents and Prime Ministers are elected to govern on the promise of bringing 'change'—often to then find reasons why change, after all, may not be as wonderful (or achievable) as promised. The way the media have used their freedoms may well have fuelled cynicism. But even allowing for this, there are plenty of legitimate reasons for Christians to have considered civil disobedience as a real option, living as we do with memories of Stalin, Mao, Pol Pot, the National Socialist Party in pre-war Germany, and any number of corrupt regimes in the East and West. And the Bible itself gives some examples of legitimate disobedience (think of Shadrach, Meshach and Abednego refusing to bow before Nebuchadnezzar's statue in Daniel 3, or the apostles insisting "We must obey God rather than men" in Acts 5:29).

However, the weight of Romans 13 falls on the obligation to obey. This is not because Paul or any of the New Testament writers were naïve about corrupt leadership. ▶

Good government

Read Romans 13:1-7.

1. What negative attitudes to government[1] and secular political leadership exist in our culture?

2. What, according to these verses, is the relationship between God and government?

3. What is the job of government?

4. Think back to the last election you voted in. It could be state, national, local or some other group to which you belong (if you do not vote, think back to the last change of 'governing authority' that affected you). What does this passage tell you about the result?

5. We are not to resist the governing authorities, but to be subject to them, and to give them their due. What does this mean in practice for us:

  a. as individuals?

  b. as a small group?

  c. as a church (cf. 1 Tim 2:1-2)?

Christians knew that the Lord Jesus himself had been crucified under the governmental authority of Herod and Pontius Pilate (Acts 4:24-28, especially v. 27). But they were also aware that even in the case of Jesus' death, earthly rulers did "whatever [God's] hand and [God's] plan had predestined to take place". Recall, too, that Paul's instructions here come only four chapters after he has spoken of God hardening Pharaoh's heart in order that God may be glorified (Rom 9:17-18). It is not that the writers of the New Testament were cynical, complacent or apathetic about government. Rather, they were firmly convinced that the great governor of every nation is God himself.

Optional question:
Consider the following verses. What do they say about a Christian attitude to government?

- Mark 12:17

- John 18:36 (cf. Dan 7:13-14)

- 1 Peter 2:13-15

Paul and the law

Paul has said that he believes God's law (meaning the Ten Commandments and the Law given through Moses to Israel) is holy, righteous and good (Rom 7:12). Even so, Paul teaches that the Law of God has significant, even fatal, limitations. So he says in the same chapter, "we serve not under the old written code but in the new life of the spirit" (Rom 7:6). He will even be so bold as to suggest that the law is toxic, bringing sin to life (Rom 7:9), and bringing about death even if the intention was to bring life (Rom 7:10).

Elsewhere, writing to the Galatians, Paul compares the law of Moses to a 'guardian', appointed to watch over God's people until the coming of Christ. "But now that faith has come, we are no longer under a guardian" (Gal 3:25). Or, as he says in Galatians 5:18: "if you are led by the Spirit, you are not under the law".

Paul could not be clearer. We are not right with God because of anything to do with the law. Although it is from God, it points away from itself and towards the fulfilment of the law in Jesus, and through him in the life of the Christian by the power of the Holy Spirit.

Read Romans 13:8-10.

6. Consider Paul's attitude to the law in these verses.

   a. What can you work out about **Paul's attitude to the law?**

   b. "Love is the fulfilling of the law", says verse 10. So how does "love" help us fulfil the law in the four specific examples Paul mentions?

   - Adultery

   - Murder

   - Covetousness

- Stealing

Read Romans 13:11-14.

7. Why does Paul warn us to "wake from sleep" (v. 11)?

8. What will 'waking from sleep' look like in practice (vv. 12-13)?

9. What are the desires of the flesh?

The righteousness of God

Commentators have spilt massive amounts of ink working out the detail of what Romans is trying to say, and they have not always come to identical conclusions. But virtually all of them agree that Romans 1:16-17 is a key to unlocking the whole letter, especially the idea that in the gospel "the righteousness of God is revealed from faith for faith". We have seen in the rest of Romans that this righteousness doesn't come about through anything we've done to win God's approval. It comes about only because when we trust in Jesus' death on the cross, we are declared 'not guilty' or 'justified' (recalling that being declared 'righteous' is the same as being 'justified'; the words in the original Greek are identical). Because God is righteous and keeps his promises, he declares us righteous through Jesus' death.

This is wonderful news, and helps us understand the *other* thing that almost all the commentators have noticed—that is, that the first eleven chapters contain almost no direct instructions (the only definite exceptions are Romans 6:11-13, 6:19, 11:18 and 11:20). However, the last five chapters are packed full of detailed instructions ▶

10. Think back over what you have read in Romans 12-13. What unique reasons do Christians have for behaving differently from everyone else? (Consider the entire section, but especially Romans 12:1-2, 12:19 and 13:11-12. Also see sidebar 'The righteousness of God'.)

›› Implications

- If someone was observing your behaviour and listening to your words, what would they conclude was your attitude to the government? Is it the attitude that Romans 13 is putting forward?

- Can you think of some areas of sin in your life, where you are making "provision for the flesh, to gratify its desires"?

- Given the relationship we have seen between life and doctrine in this study, what should you now do in order to see progress in these areas of challenge? (You may like to refer to question 10.)

on how to live the Christian life. This has nothing to do with the idea that the early part of Paul's letters are theoretical, and the later bits are practical. Paul would have scoffed at such a distinction, for there is nothing more 'practical' than getting into right relationship with the God who will one day judge us. Rather, once Paul has established what it means that "the righteousness of God is revealed" in the gospel, he moves to show how God's righteousness must lead to righteous Christian living. Back in Romans 6, he spoke of being "slaves of righteousness". Here, he urges us to "put on the Lord Jesus Christ". This is another way of saying the same thing, and emphasizes that only those who are in Christ through faith can experience God's righteousness—both in the cleansing of our guilt, and in the way we now live our lives. For more on how this works out in the lives of Christians, consider question 10.

» Give thanks and pray

- Thank God for our leaders and governments.
- Pray "for kings and all who are in high positions, that we may lead a peaceful and quiet life, godly and dignified in every way" (1 Tim 2:2).
- Thank God that he will return to judge the world.
- Pray that we will live in such a way that we will be ready for his return.

Endnote

1. Paul is undoubtedly referring to the Roman Empire, and various local expressions of the Emperor's rule, when he speaks of "governing authorities" (v. 1). But the style of government took many forms in the ancient world; likewise the wording of the verse itself means that the principles of obedience can be worked out in many different contexts—national, state, local; even down to authorities in our workplaces or community organizations. Try to think as broadly as possible, then, about how to apply Paul's instructions.

STUDY 4

FREEDOM PERFECTED

[ROMANS 14]

The Christian is free because the "law of the Spirit of life has set you free in Christ Jesus from the law of sin and death" (Rom 8:2). But we are not free to *sin*, and Paul has been at pains throughout Romans to show how becoming a Christian is the start of a *different* life, not an excuse to keep living the same old sinful life. If we live by God's mercies, then our lives are to be living sacrifices to God (Rom 12:1) and characterized by love (Rom 12:9, 13:8).

How then should we use our Christian freedom? In this study, we look at the Christian's duty to use his freedom to serve people who are 'weak' in faith. Martin Luther summarized this paradox—of being 'free' to 'serve'—with these words: "A Christian is a perfectly free lord of all, subject to none. A Christian is a perfectly dutiful servant of all, subject to all."[1] Our study of Romans 14 will help us to see how this paradox works out in practice.

Who is weak?

Paul doesn't name names in this challenging passage, leaving it up to the Romans and to us to work out exactly who is weak. But recall that in Romans 11 Paul has spoken forcefully to the Gentile Christians and warned them not to be proud that they have been included in God's people, whilst the Jews have apparently been broken off. Rather, the Gentiles are to humbly "continue in [God's] kindness. Otherwise you too will be cut off" (Rom 11:22).

Likewise, we know that Christians from a Jewish background might be tempted to pride because they have the law. Paul has spoken of such individuals back in Romans 2:17-24. They consider themselves wise because of the law of God, so that the Jew is "an instructor of the foolish". Paul warns the proud Jew that he is condemned by his hypocritical, law-breaking behaviour.

So even though Paul doesn't single out Jews or Gentiles by name, the mention of food laws almost certainly means that he has both Jewish and Gentile Christians very much in mind as he writes. That said, Christians of all sorts can easily have rules about special days, and what food and drink should be avoided—and those rules can easily become sources of conflict between believers. ▶

Not passing judgement
Read Romans 14:1-4.

1. Describe the weak person, according to these verses.

2. How would you identify a **weak** person in church today?

3. What does God think of the weak person?

4. Why should neither the weak nor the strong pass judgement on each other?

Let God be our judge

THE IDEA OF GOD'S COMING judgement against sin and sinners has been present in Romans right from chapter 1, where Paul explained how the revelation of God's righteousness is partly seen in the revelation of his *wrath* against human ungodliness and unrighteousness (Rom 1:18). The chapters that follow taught us that the Lord Jesus died to take God's judgement upon himself on the cross.

This makes God's impending judgement an ever-present reminder that our lives have been changed, and that we now stand ready to meet our judge on the final day. For Paul, this is a powerful motivator, and he has used it to remind Christians not to take vengeance upon those who do evil ("Vengeance is mine, I will repay, says the Lord"—Rom 12:19), to obey governing authorities (Rom 13:5) and to live in the light not the darkness (Rom 13:11-14).

It shouldn't surprise us, then, to find that our current chapter works this theme of God's judgement through to our behaviour and potential conflicts with fellow believers.

It may be that the rules Paul has in mind include the idea of abstaining from alcohol. However, it is important not to get sidetracked into thinking that alcohol is the major issue in the passage. After all, the 'strong' ones in this passage are the ones who don't abstain, and the 'weak' are not abstaining because of issues to do with addiction and drug abuse, but because they feel their behaviour is pleasing to the Lord.

Better present-day examples may relate to specifically religious behaviour—for example, attitudes to the Sabbath day or to reading certain novels or to celebrating certain Christian traditions. You may be able to think of other examples in your answer to question 2.

Read Romans 14:5-12.

5. Do you think Sundays, or some other day(s), are important for the Christian? Why or why not?

6. According to these verses, what is the most important reason for being convinced of your answer to question 5?

7. What is the connection between Jesus' dying and living (v. 9) and our dying and living (v. 8)? (cf. Rom 6:1-11)

8. Suppose you find yourself in a situation where you disagree with other Christians about whether to observe special days or abstain from food.

   a. Outline the principles these verses give to help work out what to do.

   b. Why mustn't we pass judgement on people who arrive at different conclusions from ours?

Not destroying the work of God

VERSES 5-12 HAVE FOCUSED ON motives for behaviour that relate to Jesus' lordship. His lordship is still very much the driving factor behind the rest of the chapter as well, but now the focus is on acting out of concern for the salvation of our brothers and sisters in Christ. This, too, is a powerful reason for changing our attitudes and our behaviour.

Read Romans 14:13-23.

9. In what way might our behaviour become a "stumbling block or hindrance" to a brother? (You may like to begin by considering relationships between Jewish and Gentile Christians—see the sidebar 'Who is weak?' on page 30.)

10. Make a list of the various reasons Paul gives for changing our behaviour.

11. Make a list of the tests we might apply to whatever behaviour we adopt.

» Implications

- What specific attitudes or actions have you been convicted about or reassured about through this passage?

- Think about your own attitude to a weak person ('weak' defined according to Romans 14).

- What temptations do you struggle with in regard to the 'weak'?

- What should your attitude be and why?

- If you are 'strong', can you think of any areas where you might need to change?

- If you are 'weak', what are your obligations to the 'strong'? Why?

» Give thanks and pray

- Thank God that he has made Jesus both Lord and Saviour.
- Ask the Lord Jesus to help you change your attitudes and actions in the light of this.
- Pray specifically about your answers under 'Implications'.

Endnote
1. Martin Luther, 'A treatise on Christian liberty (The freedom of a Christian)', in Kirsten Birkett, *The Essence of the Reformation*, 2nd edn, Matthias Media, Sydney, 2009, pp. 107-108.

STUDY 5
THE END OF WEAKNESS AND STRENGTH
[ROMANS 15:1-13]

Paul has not yet finished with his challenges to the strong and the weak. Now, however, he moves beyond the particular issues of eating, drinking and observance of special days to consider the greater and deeper reasons that lie behind the changed behaviour of all Christians. For we are not just treating each other with respect because we are members of a social club, trying to make our group life function more effectively and harmoniously. If that were true, then Christians would be no better (and no worse) than a community service organization or a sporting club. But our changed behaviour comes about because of the Lord Jesus, and in this chapter, Paul continues to show how and why this is so.

Read Romans 15:1-7.

1. If someone has a 'weaker' conscience, what should we do?

2. What is it about Christ's example that we are to imitate?

"Zeal for your house"

Paul speaks about how the Lord Jesus fulfils Psalm 69, and especially verse 9, by bearing "the reproaches of those who reproach you". In other words, Jesus did not insist on his rights, even though as the ultimate 'strong' man, fulfilling the law perfectly, he would have been entitled to do so. But it is interesting to notice that the first half of Psalm 69:9 says, "Zeal for your house has consumed me". This is quoted in John 2:17 about Jesus, just after he has angrily driven out the Jewish money-changers from God's temple in Jerusalem. The money-changers were turning God's temple into "a house of trade" (John 2:16). In the process, they were making it difficult for the Gentiles to approach God through temple worship, for the money-changers were set up in the court of the Gentiles.

So it is very fitting that Paul quotes Psalm 69 ▶

3. In verse 3, Paul quotes Psalm 69:9. Go back to this Psalm and look at verses 1-15 to get an idea of the context. What is the psalmist's predicament?

4. The psalmist prays expectantly. What does he look to God to do:

a. for himself?

b. for those who trust God?

c. to the enemies of God?

5. In quoting Psalm 69, Paul also tells us about the Old Testament and its place in the Christian life. Why is the Old Testament important? How does it help us?

6. Why do you think Paul describes God as a God of "endurance and encouragement" in verse 5?

7. *Ultimately*, what will happen if we do what Paul instructs us to do and "bear with the failings of the weak"?

as he refers to a different house—not the temple, nor any physical building, but the 'house' that God is building by gathering Jewish and Gentile believers together around his word. To be zealous for God's house will now mean not putting any stumbling blocks in the way of either Jewish or Gentile believers as they seek to honour God. As Paul urges, "Let each of us please his neighbour for his good, to build him up" (v. 2).

By speaking about how Christ behaved, and by quoting Psalm 69, Paul is multiplying reasons for us to do the right thing and look after our weaker brothers and sisters.

Read Romans 15:8-13.

8. In these verses Paul mentions the Jews ("the circumcised") and the Gentiles (that is, the non-Jews). Taking into account everything that has been said so far, which group most easily fits the category of 'weak' people, and which group most easily fits the category 'strong'? (Or if neither, explain your answer.)

9. Why did Christ become "a servant to the circumcised" (v. 8)?

Praise God!

IN VERSES 8-13, THERE ARE A RANGE of quotes from the Old Testament. If you have time, either in the group or individually, they are well worth reading carefully in context.

For the moment, however, here's a quick outline of the background behind those quotes. This will help you work out why Paul has decided to refer to these verses here in Romans 15, and in turn, the verses will uncover some profound truths about how God will be glorified.

First, in verse 9 Paul quotes Psalm 18:49. This psalm virtually reproduces 2 Samuel 22, so we have a very good idea of the historical context that the psalm refers to. It is part of a song sung by David before he has become king of Israel. He has been rescued from his enemy King Saul, and the final result is not just that David is personally grateful, though he is certainly that. Far more important in David's mind—and in the minds of all who sing the psalm—is that

God's enemies are crushed, and people from every nation end up bringing glory to God because of his righteousness. It is worth reading the psalm in your own time to feel the great weight of the glory of God as he triumphs over his enemies and establishes his rule over the whole of creation. God is king over all!

Then in verse 10, Paul quotes a song from Deuteronomy 32:43. This time the singer is another great leader of Israel, indeed the greatest of all Old Testament leaders, Moses himself. Once again, he is singing of God's universal triumph over all his enemies, even in the face of the prophesied disobedience in Israel.

Verse 11 quotes the shortest psalm in the Bible, short enough that we can reproduce it here:

> Praise the LORD, all nations!
> Extol him, all peoples!
> For great is his steadfast love toward us,
> and the faithfulness of the LORD endures forever.
> Praise the LORD! (Psalm 117)

Finally, and most important of all, Paul quotes the majestic Isaiah 11 passage where God promises that a Spirit-filled "root of Jesse" will arise to rule the nations with righteousness. Jesse was the father of David, and God had earlier promised that someone descended from David's line would sit on the throne in Jerusalem forever. Once again, the nations of the world are in view, and Paul's quote highlights that this "root of Jesse" will rule over all the Gentiles. Right at the beginning of Romans, Paul has reminded his readers that Jesus himself "was descended from David according to the flesh and was declared to be the Son of God [a royal title] in power according to the Spirit of holiness by his resurrection from the dead" (Rom 1:3-4).

10. What single message do the four Old Testament quotes in these verses spell out? You may like to write down a one sentence summary, then share your summary with the group.

11. When we hear God's Old Testament promises, as summarized here by Paul, what should our response be?

» Implications

- If you hope to be a strong Christian, what changes will you need to make based on this passage? What will bearing "with the failings of the weak" mean in practice?

- What grounds for joy, hope and peace does the Christian have that the non-Christian doesn't?

- If you don't feel hope, joy or peace, how might Paul's words in this chapter be of help over time?

- Name some specific ways in which God can be glorified through your words and actions.

» Give thanks and pray

- Thank God that Jesus did not serve himself but became a servant for our sake.
- Pray that we will follow Jesus' example and serve the 'weak'.
- Pray for opportunities to 'praise God among the Gentiles' by telling unbelievers about what God has done through the Lord Jesus.

STUDY 6
GOD BLESS AMERICA (AND EVERYONE ELSE)
[ROMANS 15:14-33]

Paul's letter to the Romans is now moving towards its conclusion. His theme throughout, clearly stated in Romans 1:17, has been the righteousness of God revealed in the gospel. Now he speaks more personally about his own vision and ambition. But because he is "a servant of Christ Jesus, called to be an apostle" (Rom 1:1), this is still relevant to his theme, for it is impossible to separate the man from his message.

It is also massively relevant to those who think of themselves as Christ's servants—namely, us. The same power of God that drives and directs Paul drives us on as well.

So although we may not exactly have the same apostolic job, which in Paul's case was to "carry my name before the Gentiles and kings and the children of Israel" (Acts 9:15), the same God has called us into his service, and the same God still intends that his name be carried "before the Gentiles …"

Not only that; if we are Gentiles, and we want to find out about our salvation, Paul is the apostle whose words and mission are most clearly for our benefit. And in this passage he very explicitly talks about the place of the Gentiles in God's plans, and his own role in bringing the gospel to them.

Paul has been bold enough to speak of "*my* gospel" (Rom 2:16). Now, in these final sections of the letter, we can learn a great deal more about the close relationship between Paul, his message, his hearers, and the God who entrusted him with that ministry. The more we read, the more those of us from the 'nations' are able to discover new insight into our own part in God's plan.

And along with this insight, we are going to discover the privileges and responsibilities—previously reserved for the Jews only—that God has given us in bringing the glory of his name to the world.

Read Romans 15:14-21.

1. What can you say about Paul's relationship to the Roman Christians (cf. Rom 1:13)?

2. In Romans 11:13, Paul has described himself as "an apostle[1] to the Gentiles". He knows this is who he is, because God himself gave Paul this job in Acts 9:15 (quoted in the introduction) and Acts 13:46-47.

   a. Considering these verses in Romans and Acts, what particular responsibilities does Paul believe God has given him?

   b. List the reasons that motivate Paul.

   c. Which of the reasons under b. are specific either to Paul or to a particular group of people (e.g. people travelling with Paul in his trips to different cities and churches)?

d. Which of the reasons under b. are ones that all Christians share?

3. In verse 16, Paul compares himself to an Old Testament priest.

a. What was the job of an Old Testament priest? (If you are unsure, there are some helpful summaries in Hebrews 5:1 and Hebrews 8:3.)

b. How then is Paul like an Old Testament priest?

c. Paul says in this verse that he is making an "offering of the Gentiles"—yet he has no physical temple or altar, and makes no literal sacrifice. So how does Paul make the offering he is referring to? (See v. 19; you may find it helpful to consider Romans 12:1, which is the other place the idea of 'sacrifice' is used.)

Isaiah and the servant

In explaining his ministry and motivation, Paul quotes the Old Testament book of Isaiah (v. 21; see question 4). It is a fascinating choice, as the passage Paul chooses is from one of what are traditionally known as the 'Servant Songs' (Isa 42:1-7, 49:1-6, 50:4-9 and 52:13-53:12). These prophecies of Isaiah feature an individual known as the 'Servant', who would bring about a great many changes that the whole Old Testament had promised and looked forward to for many long generations. Though the 'Servant' would be gentle, he would also powerfully establish justice among all the nations. He was to bring sight for the blind, freedom for prisoners and good news for the poor; his message of God's salvation would be for all the nations (not just Israel); he would therefore be revealing God's glory to all mankind. For all this, the Servant would be despised by many and suffer on account of the sins of others. Yet in the end, God would vindicate him and raise him up.

Who was this mysterious 'Servant'? Christians are in no doubt: the promises Isaiah made were fulfilled by Jesus himself. The four Gospels applied the prophecies of Isaiah to Jesus in many places— ▶

4. In verse 21, Paul quotes Isaiah 52:15.

   a. What does this verse tell us about the nature of Paul's work?

   b. By quoting this verse, what is Paul claiming about himself and his ministry (see sidebar)?

Read Romans 15:22-33.

5. Paul has several reasons for visiting Rome. What are they (cf. Rom 1:11-13)?

6. Paul says he is looking for 'help' from the Romans (v. 24). What sort of help?

7. How do Paul's words help us think about our relationship to:

   a. Jewish Christians?

   b. other Christians outside our local church?

   c. our church leaders (for example, what we pray for them)?

---

either directly (in verses such as Matthew 12:18-21, 26:67, Luke 4:17-21 and John 12:37-38) or by allusion.

For Paul to use Isaiah as he does here, then, is remarkable. Question 4 asks you to consider just how remarkable.

When you have considered question 4, you may (as an optional extra) like to reflect on Colossians 1:24 and 2 Timothy 2:10 and discuss how Paul's (and our) suffering for the gospel relates to the suffering that Christ went through.

» Implications

- In what ways is Paul's mission our mission?

- Having considered how Paul's mission is our mission, consider the practical ways suggested by Romans 15:14-33 in which *all* Christians can share in the work of spreading the gospel to those who have never heard it.

» Give thanks and pray

- Thank God for the example of Paul, Apostle to the Gentiles.
- Pray that, by our suffering, prayer and generosity, we will be able to share in reaching others with the gospel of Jesus.

Endnote
1. 'Apostle' means a 'sent one'—in this case, a person sent by God.

STUDY 7

FRIENDS AND ENEMIES

[ROMANS 16]

There are all sorts of ways to finish letters and, frankly, most of them don't require a huge amount of thought. It's the bit you put on the end when everything you want to say has been said.

Paul's letters—including the one we've been looking at—don't end this way. Some of his sentences may have been messy, and his logic so tight that you needed a microscope to find the links, but you could never accuse Paul of wasting words.

The most obvious thing about the ending of Romans is the way Paul piles on name after name of people he cares for and knows about, in a city he has never visited. Why? Is he trying to get money? Is he trying to establish credibility?

The easiest explanation is that he names the names of the people he loves and cares about because he loves and cares about them.

But let's not leave it at that. As we read on into this chapter, what we discover is that the way God's righteousness reveals itself through the gospel changes and transforms every relationship. In view of God's mercies, our thinking and our behaviour is changed (Rom 12:1-2), leading to love that is genuine (Rom 12:9). In chapter 16, we find that these are not just words poured out from the pen of a brilliant academic. Paul himself has been transformed. The very people he used to kill before he became a Christian are now the people he loves.

The other thing that we will find as we look at this chapter is that Paul never loses sight of what he has been preaching from the beginning: the righteousness of God that leads to the obedience of faith. And as he wraps up his letter, he has a warning for the Romans about those who would divert them from this faith.

Friends in the gospel
Read Romans 16:1-16, 21-23.
1. Briefly note down what Paul says about these people:

   a. Phoebe (vv. 1-2)

   b. Prisca and Aquila (vv. 3-5)

   c. Epaenetus (v. 5)

   d. Mary (v. 6)

   e. Andronicus and Junia (v. 7)

   f. Apelles (v. 10)

   g. Persis (v. 12)

   h. Rufus' mother (v. 13)

2. In all, Paul names 27 people—26 in Rome—not to mention their families. He describes four individuals as "my beloved" (the NIV has "my dear friend"), and says that Rufus' mother "has been a mother to me as well" (v. 13). He urges the members of the church to "greet one another with a holy kiss" (v. 16). What insight do these names, and the associated greetings and instructions, give into Paul's relationship with the Roman Christians (cf. 15:14 and 15:23)?

3. Elsewhere in his letters, Paul commends himself as a model for others to follow (e.g. 1 Cor 11:1; 2 Thess 3:7, 3:9; 2 Tim 3:10; cf. 2 Tim 3:14). What is worth imitating about Paul's relationship with the Roman Christians? Think specifically about:

   a. other congregation members in your church

   b. other churches you happen to be connected to (e.g. through missionaries you support)

   c. people you have particular spiritual responsibility for (e.g. family members, Bible study group members).

4. What do verses 21-23, with their mention of Paul's friends, teach us about Paul's way of doing ministry?

Enemies of the gospel

PAUL HAS SPOKEN WARMLY and at length about the gospel friends who stand beside him in the work of Christ. Perhaps it is the joy of this fellowship in the truth that prompts him to turn for a few brief verses to a problem that has hardly been mentioned previously in the letter—that is, the problem of **false teachers**.

Read Romans 16:17-20.

5. What do the false teachers do?

6. What is their motive?

How to treat false teachers

These days, we tend to find talk about 'false teachers' a bit strange and hard to deal with. In our age of tolerance, to simply dismiss people in the way that Paul does in verses 17-18 would be seen as arrogant and outrageous. Three things stand out in these two verses.

Firstly, paying attention to what a man is saying or teaching is going to be a part of recognizing his sinfulness. In Romans 3:10-18, Paul diagnoses the human condition painfully well: it's throats, tongues, lips and mouths that cause great damage—damage as great as any other body parts are capable of doing. His thought parallels what James writes to remind his readers that "the tongue is a fire, a world of unrighteousness" (Jas 3:6). So if we are trying to recognize "those who cause divisions and create obstacles", we need to know thoroughly "the doctrine that you have been taught". ▶

7. What should the Romans do to counter their threat (vv. 17, 19)?

8. What has Paul done to help them counter the threat?

9. What will God do to help them with the threat?

Secondly, Paul is unembarrassed about attacking the character of the false teachers. He simply describes what they are like. They don't really serve the Lord Jesus, they follow their own appetites, they use smooth talk, they are flatterers, they deceive the naive, they sell their grandmothers, they loiter around schoolyards and take photos using mobile phones, and so on (those last two may be exaggerations). It takes real courage and honesty to speak like this, but Paul has it. May the Lord Jesus grant the same to us.

Thirdly, Paul's exhortation to "avoid them" goes strongly against the spirit of our age, where debate and discussion are seen as ends in themselves. According to Paul, there comes a time when dialogue, debate and the free interchange of ideas are positively harmful.

THERE IS NOTHING IN THESE VERSES that helps identify exactly what the false teachers believed, except that it was contrary to the apostolic doctrine the Romans had been taught. Douglas Moo summarizes neatly: "Identifying these false teachers is nearly impossible."[1] Paul's fundamental concern, though, is doctrinal in nature. We see this in two ways.

Firstly, because the people Paul is concerned about are labelled *false teachers*. There were questions about their morality, and Paul's description hints at this. But this is not fundamentally how the people concerned are designated. It is the falsehood of their teaching that is the root problem.

Secondly, we see Paul's concern reflected in his view that these teachers "create obstacles contrary to the *doctrine that you have been taught*" (v. 17).

With these words, Paul effectively reminds readers of the importance of everything he's been saying in the entire letter. So, because we have now reached the end of Romans, let's summarize.

STUDY 7 FRIENDS AND ENEMIES » 55

Optional exercise

Spend 15 or 20 minutes dividing the letter amongst the group, perhaps giving one or two chapters to each group member. Note down the key issues raised in each chapter of the letter up to and including 16:16. Use the table below to summarize your findings. Romans 9 and 16 have been filled in as examples.

Romans chapter	Key issues dealt with (no less than one, no more than three)
1	1. 2. 3.
2	1. 2. 3.
3	1. 2. 3.
4	1. 2. 3.
5	1. 2. 3.
6	1. 2. 3.
7	1. 2. 3.
8	1. 2. 3.
9	1. What about (physical) Israel, for whom Paul is in anguish? 2. The overriding importance of the glory of God. 3. God gives righteousness by faith.

Romans chapter	Key issues dealt with (no less than one, no more than three)
10	1. 2. 3.
11	1. 2. 3.
12	1. 2. 3.
13	1. 2. 3.
14	1. 2. 3.
15	1. 2. 3.
16:1-16	1. Paul's love for the "beloved" Romans he knows. 2. 3.

Looking at the overall content of Romans, what has Paul said that will help his readers respond to false teachers?

The obedience of faith

If you are ever trying to get a sense of what a letter or a book is about, one tried and tested strategy is to read the beginning and then go straight to the end, to see where the author himself thinks he is heading. By that method you will often find important clues as to what the writer thought he was on about.

In the case of Romans, notice especially Paul's repeated expression: "the obedience of faith". It's there in the very last sentence of Romans; it's also right back at the beginning of Romans in verse 5 of chapter 1. That one little phrase, "the obedience of faith", could almost summarize Paul's entire message. What he has been trying to do by preaching Christ and the righteousness of God is to produce in his readers "the obedience of faith", as their lives are transformed through the mercies of God (remember Romans 12:1).

But what exactly does Paul mean?

Does "obedience of faith" mean that the whole of Christian obedience is completely summed up and satisfied when we put our faith in the Lord Jesus? So that, in other words, the "obedience of faith" is the obedience that *consists* of faith? That is certainly consistent with everything Paul has taught in Romans, especially in Romans 1:17 (the topic sentence of the letter) where "the righteousness of God is revealed from faith for faith".

Or alternatively does "the obedience of faith" mean the obedience that *results* from faith? That is, if you have faith, that faith will express itself in a life of love and obedience to the Lord Jesus. Again, when we read Romans, this message is unmistakable. It is especially clear in passages like Romans 6, where to become a Christian is to "become obedient from the heart to the standard of teaching to which you were committed" (Rom 6:17).

The most sensible and helpful option is to say that Paul meant to say both. Any ambiguity in the expression is not accidental, but deliberate. For both ideas are undoubtedly taught in Romans. And Paul's repetition of "the obedience of faith" at the beginning and end of the letter has given him a perfect way of summarizing both. To be a Christian is to have faith in Christ, for that is what obedience looks like. But to be a Christian and to have faith in Christ is to express that faith in obedience, for, as James 2:26 puts it, "faith apart from works is dead".

So as we finish Romans, let's pray that we might have "the obedience of faith".

» Implications

- How can you bring about "the obedience of faith" (1:5, 16:26) in yourself and others?

- "It's all about you." What evidence is there in Romans, especially in the final verses, to suggest that this is a falsehood?

- How does Romans help us respond to false teachers?

- Looking back over your study of Romans, what are the main things you have learned?

» Give thanks and pray

- Thank God for revealing his righteousness in the death and resurrection of Jesus.
- Pray that we, being transformed by God's mercy, may not be conformed to the world, but offer our bodies as living sacrifices, holy and acceptable to God (Rom 12:1).

> **Feedback on this resource**
>
> We really appreciate getting feedback about our resources—not just suggestions for how to improve them, but also positive feedback and ways they can be used. We especially love to hear that the resources may have helped someone in their Christian growth.
>
> You can send feedback to us via the 'Feedback' menu in our online store, or write to us at PO Box 225, Kingsford NSW 2032, Australia.

Endnote
1. Douglas Moo, *The Epistle to the Romans*, The New International Commentary on the New Testament, Eerdmans, Grand Rapids, 1996, p. 929.

Matthias Media is an evangelical publishing ministry that seeks to persuade all Christians of the Bible-shaped, theological truth of God's purposes in Jesus Christ, and equip them with high-quality resources, so that they will:

- abandon their lives to the honour and service of Christ in daily holiness and decision-making
- pray constantly in Christ's name for the growth of his gospel
- speak the Bible's life-changing word whenever and however they can—in the home, in the world and in the fellowship of his people.

It was in 1988 that we first started pursuing this mission, and in God's kindness we now have more than 300 different ministry resources being used all over the world. These resources range from Bible studies and books through to training courses and audio sermons.

To find out more about our large range of very useful resources, and to access samples and free downloads, visit our website:

www.matthiasmedia.com.au

How to buy our resources

1. Direct from us over the internet:
   - in the US: www.matthiasmedia.com
   - in Australia and the rest of the world: www.matthiasmedia.com.au

2. Direct from us by phone:
   - in the US: 1 866 407 4530
   - in Australia: 1800 814 360
     (Sydney: 9663 1478)
   - international: +61-2-9663-1478

3. Through a range of outlets in various parts of the world. Visit **www.matthiasmedia.com.au/international.php** for details about recommended retailers in your part of the world, including www.thegoodbook.co.uk in the United Kingdom.

4. Trade enquiries can be addressed to:
   - in the US and Canada: sales@matthiasmedia.com
   - in Australia and the rest of the world: sales@matthiasmedia.com.au

Register at our website for our **free** regular email update to receive information about the latest new resources, **exclusive special offers**, and free articles to help you grow in your Christian life and ministry.

Other Interactive and Topical Bible Studies from Matthias Media

Our Interactive Bible Studies (IBS) and Topical Bible Studies (TBS) are a valuable resource to help you keep feeding from God's word. The IBS series works through passages and books of the Bible; the TBS series pulls together the Bible's teaching on topics such as money or prayer. As at February 2009, the series contains the following titles:

Beyond Eden
GENESIS 1-11
Authors: Phillip Jensen and Tony Payne, 9 studies

Out of Darkness
EXODUS 1-18
Author: Andrew Reid, 8 studies

The Shadow of Glory
EXODUS 19-40
Author: Andrew Reid, 7 studies

The One and Only
DEUTERONOMY
Author: Bryson Smith, 8 studies

The Good, the Bad and the Ugly
JUDGES
Author: Mark Baddeley, 10 studies

Famine and Fortune
RUTH
Authors: Barry Webb and David Höhne, 4 studies

Renovator's Dream
NEHEMIAH
Authors: Phil Campbell and Greg Clarke, 7 studies

The Eye of the Storm
JOB
Author: Bryson Smith, 6 studies

The Search for Meaning
ECCLESIASTES
Author: Tim McMahon, 9 studies

Two Cities
ISAIAH
Authors: Andrew Reid and Karen Morris, 9 studies

Kingdom of Dreams
DANIEL
Authors: Andrew Reid and Karen Morris, 9 studies

Burning Desire
OBADIAH AND MALACHI
Authors: Phillip Jensen and Richard Pulley, 6 studies

Warning Signs
JONAH
Author: Andrew Reid, 6 studies

On That Day
ZECHARIAH
Author: Tim McMahon, 8 studies

Full of Promise
THE BIG PICTURE OF THE O.T.
Authors: Phil Campbell and Bryson Smith, 8 studies

The Good Living Guide
MATTHEW 5:1-12
Authors: Phillip Jensen and Tony Payne, 9 studies

News of the Hour
MARK
Authors: Peter Bolt and Tony Payne, 10 studies

Proclaiming the Risen Lord
LUKE 24-ACTS 2
Author: Peter Bolt, 6 studies

Mission Unstoppable
ACTS
Author: Bryson Smith, 10 studies

The Free Gift of Life
ROMANS 1-5
Author: Gordon Cheng, 8 studies

The Free Gift of Sonship
ROMANS 6-11
Author: Gordon Cheng, 8 studies

The Freedom of Christian Living
ROMANS 12-16
Author: Gordon Cheng, 7 studies

Free for All
GALATIANS
Authors: Phillip Jensen and Kel Richards, 8 studies

Walk this Way
EPHESIANS
Author: Bryson Smith, 8 studies

Partners for Life
PHILIPPIANS
Author: Tim Thorburn, 8 studies

The Complete Christian
COLOSSIANS
Authors: Phillip Jensen and Tony Payne, 8 studies

To the Householder
1 TIMOTHY
Authors: Phillip Jensen and Greg Clarke, 9 studies

Run the Race
2 TIMOTHY
Author: Bryson Smith, 6 studies

The Path to Godliness
TITUS
Authors: Phillip Jensen and Tony Payne, 7 studies

From Shadow to Reality
HEBREWS
Author: Joshua Ng, 10 studies

The Implanted Word
JAMES
Authors: Phillip Jensen and Kirsten Birkett, 8 studies

Homeward Bound
1 PETER
Authors: Phillip Jensen and Tony Payne, 10 studies

All You Need to Know
2 PETER
Author: Bryson Smith, 6 studies

The Vision Statement
REVELATION
Author: Greg Clarke, 9 studies

Bold I Approach
PRAYER
Author: Tony Payne, 6 studies

Cash Values
MONEY
Author: Tony Payne, 5 studies

The Blueprint
DOCTRINE
Authors: Phillip Jensen and Tony Payne, 9 studies

Woman of God
THE BIBLE ON WOMEN
Author: Terry Blowes, 8 studies

Tools for studying Romans

You've just finished our Interactive Bible Study on Romans 12-16. If you'd like to study the rest of Romans—whether in detail, at a simpler level, or by listening to sermons—we have the tools you need.

Learning by doing: Interactive Bible Studies

The Free Gift of Life
8 studies on Romans 1-5

This is the first in our set of Interactive Bible Studies on Romans. In *The Free Gift of Life*, Gordon Cheng shows how Romans can change everything for you. Learn from the passage that Martin Luther said is "the chief point, and the very central place of the epistle, and of the whole Bible".

The Free Gift of Sonship
8 studies on Romans 6-11

The Free Gift of Sonship is your guide to the riches of Romans 6-11. You'll delve into the personally challenging teaching about obedience and righteousness in chapter 6; the demanding discussion about whether God has kept his promises to Israel in chapters 9-11; and the majestic teaching of chapter 8 regarding the Spirit, the Christian life and the hope of glory.

Learning by listening: Romans on CD/MP3

20 talks by Phillip Jensen

Phillip Jensen, one of Australia's most incisive preachers, looks at the difficult details in Romans, and helps us to understand and appreciate the book of which Calvin said, "When any one gains a knowledge of this epistle, he has an entrance opened to him to all the most hidden treasures of Scripture".

FOR MORE INFORMATION OR TO ORDER CONTACT:

Matthias Media
Telephone: +61-2-9663-1478
Facsimile: +61-2-9663-3265
Email: info@matthiasmedia.com.au
Internet: www.matthiasmedia.com.au

Matthias Media (USA)
Telephone: 1-866-407-4530
Facsimile: 724-964-8166
Email: sales@matthiasmedia.com
Internet: www.matthiasmedia.com

Getting the whole picture: an overview of Romans

Peace with God
9 studies on Romans

This set of simple studies takes us through the key passages in the letter in nine studies, and shows us the great saving power of the God in whom we trust.

Newcomers to Romans will have the entire scope of the book laid out before them, with the key landmarks shown in depth and clarity. And those who are more familiar with Romans will find these studies a refreshing look at the gospel that brings us peace with God.

Leader's notes included.

About Pathway Bible Guides

Pathway Bible Guides are simple, straightforward, easy-to-read Bible studies, ideal for groups who are new to studying the Bible, or groups with limited time for study. We've designed the studies to be short and easy to use, with an uncomplicated vocabulary. At the same time, we've tried to do justice to the passages being studied, and to model good Bible-reading principles. Pathway Bible Guides are simple without being simplistic; no-nonsense without being no-content.

As at February 2009, the series contains the following titles:

- *Beginning with God* (Genesis 1-12)
- *Getting to Know God* (Exodus 1-20)
- *The Art of Living* (Proverbs)
- *Seeing Things God's Way* (Daniel)
- *Fear and Freedom* (Matthew 8-12)
- *Following Jesus* (Luke 9-12)
- *Peace with God* (Romans)
- *Church Matters* (1 Corinthians 1-7)
- *Standing Firm* (1 Thessalonians)

FOR MORE INFORMATION OR TO ORDER CONTACT:

Matthias Media
Telephone: +61-2-9663-1478
Facsimile: +61-2-9663-3265
Email: info@matthiasmedia.com.au
Internet: www.matthiasmedia.com.au

Matthias Media (USA)
Telephone: 1-866-407-4530
Facsimile: 724-964-8166
Email: sales@matthiasmedia.com
Internet: www.matthiasmedia.com